BUNGALOWS

AND

COUNTRY RESIDENCES.

Also by RA Briggs in JM Classic Editions
Homes for the Country

BUNGALOWS

AND

COUNTRY RESIDENCES

A SERIES OF DESIGNS, AND EXAMPLES
OF EXECUTED WORKS

BY

R. A. BRIGGS, ARCHITECT, F.R.I.B.A.
(Soane Medallist)

Fifth Edition, Revised, with several New Plates

JM

CLASSIC EDITIONS

This edition digitally re-mastered and
published by JM Classic Editions © 2007
Original text © RA Briggs 1901

ISBN 978-1-905217-69-4

PREFACE.

— —•— —

IT is very gratifying to me to find that the call for successive editions of this work justifies the intention of its first publication. Each of the three preceding editions has been enlarged by the introduction of extra plates, but the present is altered to such an extent as to require something more than its precursors in the way of Foreword.

In order to give as much variety as possible, not only in the designs themselves, but also in the cost of the actual buildings (which ranges from £400 to £11,000), I have made a further selection from my sketches, and have carefully revised the whole of the estimates, bringing up to date those of such houses as have been built, by allowances on the contract prices for the increased cost of labour and materials which has occurred since they were erected. It may be well to point out to persons about to build, that a room more or less can generally be added or omitted without altering the idea of the design.

As to the Country Houses, the plans and views speak for themselves, but I may say that my aim has been to show that small houses, costing about £1,000, can be built simply, economically, and, I hope it will be thought, artistically. My work will not have been in vain if it demonstrates that such houses, which would let for about £80 or £90 per annum, can each have its own individuality, and that it is not necessary that cheap houses should be distinctive only by their ugliness and vulgarity. Unfortunately, although the general design of a house may be artistic in outline, it is important to remember, that unless it is carried out under the supervision of an able architect, the design and execution of its details may be so bad as to utterly ruin the original conception, as the general effect depends very largely on the contours of mouldings and their artistic rendering.

A Country House differs from a Bungalow in that more Reception Rooms, and Rooms of a larger size, must be provided, with accommodation for visitors and their entertainment, and that the style of the architecture must suggest greater stability. In planning both Bungalows and Houses an important factor to be borne in mind is the economical working of the house. The Dining Room should always be placed near the Kitchen, so that meals may be quickly served, and although the Pantry should be near both these Rooms, it should be in the nearest possible proximity to the Entrance. In most of the plans illustrated, a good-sized Hall is provided, which can be used as a Sitting Room. The Entrance should as often as possible be placed away from the Garden, so that the pleasure grounds may have greater seclusion. With regard to aspect, the Dining Room should be arranged so that the morning sun can enter, and the Drawing Room should receive the afternoon and evening light.

And now for a word about Bungalows and Bungalow Houses. What is a Bungalow?

A Bungalow in England has come to mean neither the sun-proof squat house of India, nor the rough log hut of colder regions. It is not necessarily a one-storied building, nor is it a country cottage. A Bungalow essentially is a little "nook" or "retreat." A Cottage is a little house in the country, but a Bungalow is a little country house—a homely, cosy little place, with verandahs and balconies, and the plan so arranged as to ensure complete comfort, with a feeling of rusticity and ease. Cheapness and economy are important factors, but they should not be obtained at the cost of substantiality and utility. Our climate is not so hot, nor our sun so scorching, that we can dispense with its rays nor can land be bought in England for the proverbial "song," so as to allow of a Bungalow containing many rooms being built in one storey. We have also to consider the Bye-Laws of the Local Authorities, and the fact that wood, bricks, and labour must be paid for. In England too, we must have our roofs so constructed that the rain-water can easily get away, and although we can have balconies and verandahs, we must allow the sunlight to enter our rooms. It is cheaper also to have a house of two storeys with the bedrooms partly in the roof, than to have all the rooms on one floor. A most important point is that of the sanitary arrangements, which must of course receive great attention, and in the cheapest Bungalow the most approved system must be adopted.

With all these conditions, however, Bungalows are very cheap in comparison with Houses, as the great aim in the designs being simplicity, the planning may be somewhat different; and the walls, too, may be built of wood, where allowed by the Local Authorities. On this account Bungalows are very popular, and appeal especially to people of moderate means, or to those who would seek the rest of a quiet week-end, "far from the madding crowd," whose "ignoble strife" compels their work-a-day attendance. A House in the country with its attendant expenses would be beyond their means, but a Bungalow can be built and maintained at a comparatively trifling cost.

Bungalows, if they are built of stud-walls, can be covered outside either with tiles or weather boarding, creosoted, or stained and varnished, or oiled; or they may be "rough cast." Inside, the walls should be plastered. Brick is also available, but experience tells us that it is warmer and drier in winter, and cooler in summer, to have stud-walls covered in the manner described, than to have thin brick walls. The roofs can be tiled either with the ordinary flat tiles, or with patent pantiles, which give a pleasing effect. They can also be thatched, where allowed. Where the walls are built of brick, they can be 9 in. walls, tiled or rough cast, but this somewhat increases the expense. Great variety can be obtained in the planning, and a very useful and economical arrangement is the Hall-Sitting Room. This does away with a great amount of passage space, and it should be borne in mind that passages, except for the purpose of giving access to rooms, are all waste. The Hall-Sitting Room can be made a most effective feature, and it can be used for a variety of purposes. Large verandahs and balconies can be arranged, but as a rule, one window in each room should have direct light. Large bow windows can also be contrived, as they have the advantage of the verandah, but being under cover are more suitable to our uncertain climate.

Whether a Bungalow or a House be erected, great care should be taken in laying out the Gardens immediately around the House, and attention should be given even to the smallest details, such as gates and fences. What lends so great a charm to many of the old Country Houses is their gardens; their high privet hedges giving a shelter from the cold winds; their "Formal" gardens, with their box borders and gravel paths laid out in geometrical patterns; their yews cut and clipped in fantastical forms; a terrace for a stroll; a rustic summerhouse for a book; all quaint, picturesque, and charming. And if the walls of the Bungalows be covered with creepers of jasmine and roses, and the little gardens filled with old-fashioned sweet-smelling flowers, its owner may look round, and say with Herrick :—

> "Here we rejoyce, because no rent
> We pay for our poore tenement;
> And bless our fortunes when we see
> Our own beloved privacie."

R. A. BRIGGS, F.R.I.B.A.

AMBERLEY HOUSE,
   12, NORFOLK STREET, STRAND,
     June, 1901.

DESCRIPTION OF PLATES.

PLATE I.—This design is for a Bungalow which might be built in a hilly district, as shown on the drawing, the effect being gained by the simplicity of the design. The walls would be of brick, faced with rubble or rough cast, and the roofs thatched. A Hall-Sitting Room is provided, which is an economical arrangement of plan, as it obviates the necessity of long passages and would be used as a General Sitting Room. The Bedrooms would be cut off by a door into the passage giving access to them, which is a necessary arrangement for Bungalows on one floor. The woodwork would be painted white throughout, except the outside louvre shutters, which would be painted bright green. The estimated cost is £600.

PLATE II.—This is an illustration of a cheap Bungalow built in Surrey, with the two end Bedrooms omitted—thus providing three Bedrooms. The walls are of stud-work covered with felt and weather-boarding, oiled, stained, and varnished, on dwarf brick walls; and as the latter have a proper damp-proof course, any chance of damp rising is obviated. This form of construction has shown that it is warmer in winter than an ordinary 9 in. brick wall, and cooler in summer. The roofs are tiled, and the walls inside are plastered. The whole of the woodwork, except the weather-boarding, is painted ivory white. The estimated cost is £400.

PLATE III.—This is a design for a Bungalow on one floor. The walls would be built with rubble or bricks, or they might be "rough-cast," the arches to the Piazza being of red bricks, and the voussoirs of the principal entrance being of stone. The chimneys also would be faced with stone and the roofs would be tiled. The woodwork generally would be painted white, the shutters to the windows and the entrance door being bright green. The estimated cost is £800.

PLATE IV.—This is an illustration of a small Bungalow-House in the style of the Boer Houses in South Africa. It is proposed that the walls should be rough cast. The estimated cost is about £1,300. A useful feature in the plan is the moveable folding screen which would allow of the Drawing Room and Hall being thrown into one on special occasions, thus forming one large room.

PLATE V. shows a design for a Bungalow-House, which is cruciform on plan, and which, with a few slight alterations, has been built at Ewell. The walls up to the first-floor level were faced with red bricks; the walls to the first-floor and the roofs were tiled. The woodwork was painted white. The estimated cost is £1,300.

PLATES VI. and VII.—These plates show illustrations of a Bungalow-House which was designed to be built in Surrey. Advantage was taken of the fall of the ground so that the principal floor, containing the Reception Rooms and Best Bedrooms should be about 10 ft.

above the ground at the lowest point. A verandah runs nearly round the House, from which magnificent views would have been obtained. The feature of the House is the large Hall, 55 ft. by 18 ft. which would be used as a Dining Room and for general purposes. PLATE VII. shows a view of this room with its open timber roof, clerestory, and bow windows, ingle-nook, and high dado panelling. At the south end of the Hall is a Minstrels' Gallery, to which a turret staircase gives access, as well as to the Smoking Room on the lower floor. The walls to the lower floor would be of brick faced with stone, the remainder being stud-walls, covered with tiles and "half-timber" work. The roofs would be tiled. The estimated cost is £3,300.

PLATE VIII.—This is an illustration of a Bungalow-House in the same style as that shown by Plate IV. The feature of this Bungalow is the long Hall, being, as in the Boer houses, taken through the middle of the House. Moveable glass screens and doors would be placed between this Hall and the Drawing Room, so that a very large room could be so obtained. The estimated cost is about £3,100.

PLATE IX.—This is a design founded on one for a Bungalow built in Surrey. The ground floor walls are of brick, and the first floor walls are of stud-work covered with tiles. The estimated cost is £700.

PLATES X. and XI. show a design for a Bungalow in a free Greek style, giving, in an economical way, an individuality to a cheap class of building. The walls would be faced with local stone or "rough cast," and the roof covered with patent pantiles. The cost of this Bungalow would be about £1,400.

PLATE XII.—The Bungalow-House illustrated by this plate was designed to be built at Hampstead, and is somewhat similar in style to the Bungalow shown on Plates XVIII. and XIX. Eight bedrooms will be provided; the estimated cost is £2,700.

PLATE XIII.—This is an illustration of a House that was built on a site at Marlow, overlooking the River Thames. The walls were faced with red bricks, the roof was tiled, and the woodwork throughout was painted white. The estimated cost of the House is about £2,800.

PLATE XIV.—Is an illustration of a House which has lately been built at Farnborough, Surrey, at a cost of £3,000. The walls up to the first floor level are faced with red local bricks, and the "dressings" are of "Monk's Park" Stone. The walls to the first floor are "rough cast." The roofs are tiled and the half-timber work, barge boards, etc., are of teak. The Hall is carried up two storeys, having a gallery round.

PLATES XV. XVI. and XVII.—This Bungalow has been built at Bellagio, Surrey, as a bachelors' summer residence. The Hall-Sitting Room is used as a Dining and Drawing Room. Plate XVII. shows the interior with the small gallery and ingle-nook of oak, stained dark. The whole of the windows are filled with lead lights, and the woodwork throughout is stained dark brown. A verandah runs nearly round the whole Bungalow, and the roof is thatched. The space contained by the stone dwarf walls is now used only as cellarage, but at a small expense it could be converted into rooms. The estimated cost of the building is £1,100.

PLATES XVIII. and XIX. show a Bungalow-House which has been built at Northwood. The whole of the rooms on the first floor are in the Mansard roof—a cheap form of construction—and although one wall to each roof is sloping, it can be fitted with cupboards, etc., which would hide the slope, if considered a defect. The roof is covered with boarding, felt and tiles, which render the rooms cool in summer and warm in winter. Particular care should be taken to lay out the garden in the "old Italian fashion" with pleasaunces, etc., formed with high yew and privet hedges. The estimated cost of this House is about £1,400.

PLATES XX. and XXI.—This is a design for a Bungalow-House with the ground floor walls faced with stone, and the first floor walls covered with "half-timber" work. The principal feature is the Hall, carried up two floors in height, and having an enriched plaster ceiling. An arcaded corridor, giving access to the bedrooms, runs completely round, thus greatly economizing space, and giving a picturesque effect to the Hall, shown on Plate XXI. The woodwork would be stained dark as old oak. An ingle-nook is planned in the Dining Room, and a verandah runs the whole length of the building. The estimated cost is £2,200.

PLATE XXII. This Bungalow-House has been built in Surrey, with certain alterations. The walls to the ground floor are faced with red bricks, and those to the first floor of stud-work, cemented, and "rough cast." The estimated cost is £1,000.

PLATE XXIII. shows a Bungalow-House which has been built at Crowborough, Sussex. It contains four Reception Rooms, and four Bedrooms, Hall, Bathroom and Kitchen Offices. The walls were faced with local stone and the roofs were tiled. The whole of the woodwork was stained dark brown and varnished. Inside the walls were plastered. The estimated cost of the House is about £1,700.

PLATES XXIV. and XXV.—This is a design for a small House, suitable for a low-lying and flat country. The estimated cost is £700. Plate XXV. shows the treatment of the Sitting-Room Hall, ingle-nook and staircase. The woodwork was painted white.

PLATE XXVI.—This is the Garden Front of a House which has been built at Hamble. The design is somewhat similar to that illustrated by Plates XVIII. and XIX. The estimated cost is £1,800.

PLATE XXVII. is a design for a House economically built at Sutton. The estimated cost of it is £1,100. The walls to the ground floor are 16 in. hollow walls faced with red bricks, and those to the first floor 9 in. covered, as the roof, with tiles. The whole of the woodwork is stained dark brown and oiled, and the windows filled with leaded lights.

PLATE XXVIII.—This House has been built at Northwood, and is similar in design to Plates XVIII. and XIX. The estimated cost is £1,100.

PLATE XXIX.—This pair of Houses was built at Burnt Ash Hill, Lee. The walls to the ground floor were faced with red bricks, the walls to the first floor being "rough-cast." The roofs were tiled and the woodwork was stained dark brown. The estimated cost is £2,700 for the pair.

PLATE XXX.—This is an illustration of a pair of semi-detached Houses which were designed for a plot of ground where the space was somewhat limited. There are four Bedrooms and two Attics to each House. The estimated cost of the Houses is £3,000 for the pair.

PLATES XXXI. and XXXII.—This is a design for a House which has been built on an acre plot of land near London, and contains accommodation much in request for Houses to be let at about £120 per annum. The walls to the ground floor were faced with red bricks, and those to the first floor, together with the roof, were hung with tiles. The gables, of half-timber work, have been introduced to form a contrast to the red tiles and bricks. The upper lights of the windows were filled with clear leaded glass. The estimated cost of the House is £1,800.

PLATES XXXIII. and XXXIV.—These are illustrations of the Entrance and Garden Fronts of a House which was built at Harrow-on-the-Hill. The Hall was carried up two storeys with a gallery round, and was similar to the Hall shown on Plate XXI. Six Bedrooms, a Dressing and Bath Room, with W.C., etc., were provided on the first floor. The walls to the ground floor, the Entrance and Dining Room with Bedroom over, were faced externally with red bricks, and had Monks Park stone dressings ; the rest of the walls were covered with tiles or half-timber work, as shown in the illustrations. The whole of the woodwork was stained dark brown and oiled. The estimated cost is £2,800.

PLATE XXXV.—This is an illustration of the Garden Front of a House that has been built at Welwyn, Herts. The walls externally throughout are faced with red bricks and the roofs are tiled with dark red tiles. The woodwork throughout is painted white. The estimated cost is £3,100.

PLATE XXXVI. shows the front view of a House that was built at Woodford, Essex. The dressings to the windows and porch were of Bath stone, and the walls were faced with red bricks. The roofs were slated with green slates, and the woodwork outside was painted white. The estimated cost of the House is £3,000.

PLATES XXXVII. and XXXVIII. show illustrations of a House with its walls either built or covered entirely with half-timber work. The design was founded on that of Bramhall Hall, and was made for a gentleman who is a member of the family who owned and inhabited this fine old mansion. The woodwork would be stained dark brown and oiled, the roofs would be tiled. Plate XXXVII. shows the Entrance Front, and Plate XXXVIII. the Garden Front. The estimated cost is £2,300.

PLATE XXXIX.—This is a design for a House in the 18th-century Renaissance style. Great uniformity is aimed at, the simplicity and proportions of the design being more considered than elaborate ornament. The walls would be faced with red bricks, and the dressings would be of stone. The roof would be tiled. The Entrance Gates and Piers, giving great stateliness to the approach, are a particular feature of this style. The estimated cost for the House is about £3,800.

PLATE XL. shows the design of a House which would have its walls to the ground-floor faced with red bricks, those to the first floor being covered either with tiles or " half-timber " work. The two circular bay windows to Drawing Room and Bedrooms over would be " rough cast." The roofs would be tiled. There are nine Bedrooms, a Dressing Room and Bathroom, etc., on the first floor. The estimated cost is £6,000.

PLATE XLI.—This is a design for a House to be faced with stone. The Hall will be carried up two floors in height, and considerable effect will be gained by the staircase and arcaded corridor opening into it. The Dining and Drawing Rooms could be thrown into one by folding doors, as both rooms open into the Vestibule. The House was designed to be built on a site having a considerable fall, and advantage has been taken of it by placing the Butler's Pantries, Housekeeper's Room, facing the garden, and the Kitchen Offices facing the back, on the lower level. It was proposed that the fittings to the Hall and Reception Rooms should be of oak. Ten Bedrooms will be provided. The estimated cost is £6,000.

PLATES XLII. and XLIII. show the Entrance and Garden Fronts of a House that was built near Limpsfield, Surrey. The walls to the ground floor were faced with red bricks, the dressings to the Hall, Staircase and Entrance porch being of " Monk's Park " stone. The walls to the first floor were covered with tiles and " half-timber " work, as may be seen from the illustration. The roofs were tiled. The woodwork was stained dark brown. The estimated cost of the House is about £4,000.

PLATES XLIV. and XLV. illustrates the Entrance and Garden Fronts of a House which has been built near Leamington. The whole of the dressings are of red Penkridge stone, and the walls are faced with red local bricks. The Hall, Parlour and Dining Room are panelled in oak. The estimated cost of this House is £5,000.

PLATES XLVI. and XLVII. illustrates the Entrance and Garden Fronts of a House designed to be built in Devonshire. It was proposed that the walls should be faced with local stone and that the roofs should be slated. The principal Reception Rooms would have been panelled in oak, and the ceilings would have had plaster enrichments. The estimated cost of this House is about £11,000.

Plate I.

Plate II

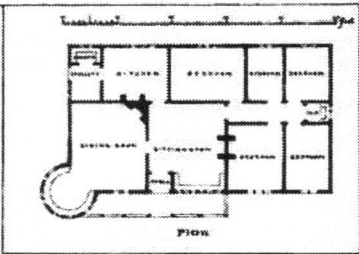

Plate III

Plate IV

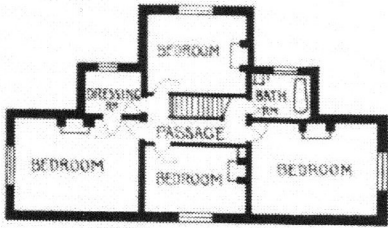

FIRST FLOOR PLAN

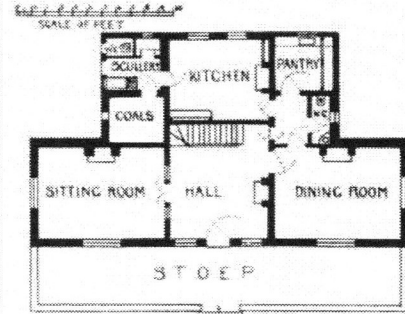

BEDROOM

DRESSING RM

BATH RM

PASSAGE

BEDROOM

BEDROOM

BEDROOM

SCALE OF FEET

SCULLERY

KITCHEN

PANTRY

COALS

SITTING ROOM

HALL

DINING ROOM

S T O E P

GROUND FLOOR PLAN

1901

Plate V

Plate VI.

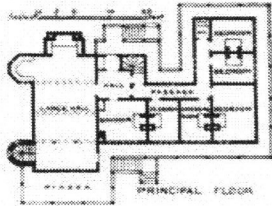

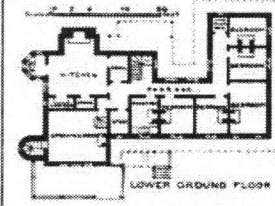

Plate VII.

Plate VIII.

FIRST FLOOR PLAN

GROUND FLOOR PLAN

SCALE OF FEET

1907

J. Akerman Photo-lith London

Plate IX

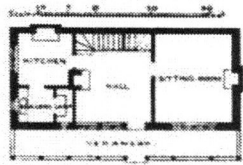

GROUND FLOOR PLAN

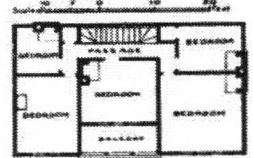

FIRST FLOOR PLAN

Plate X

GROUND FLOOR PLAN

FIRST FLOOR PLAN

J. Akerman, Photo-lith London

Plate XI.

J. Akerman, photo-lith. London.

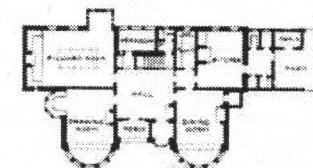

Plate XII.

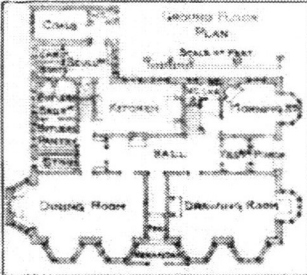

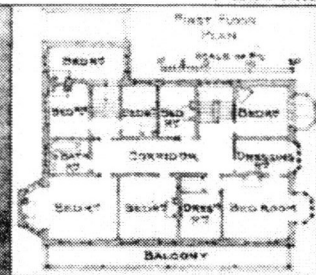

Plate XIII

Plate XIV.

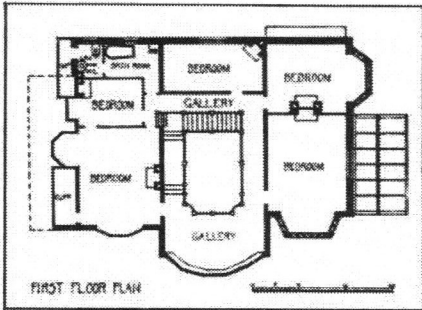

FIRST FLOOR PLAN

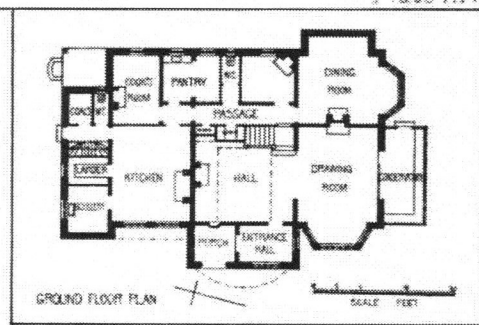

GROUND FLOOR PLAN

SCALE FEET

Plate XV.

The Garden Front

Plate XVI

The Side

Scale of [feet]

PLAN

SCULLERY
KITCHEN
HALL
C PASS
BEDROOM
BEDROOM
DINING ROOM
BEDROOM
BEDROOM
GALLERY OVER
VERANDAH

J. Akerman. Photo. Lith. London

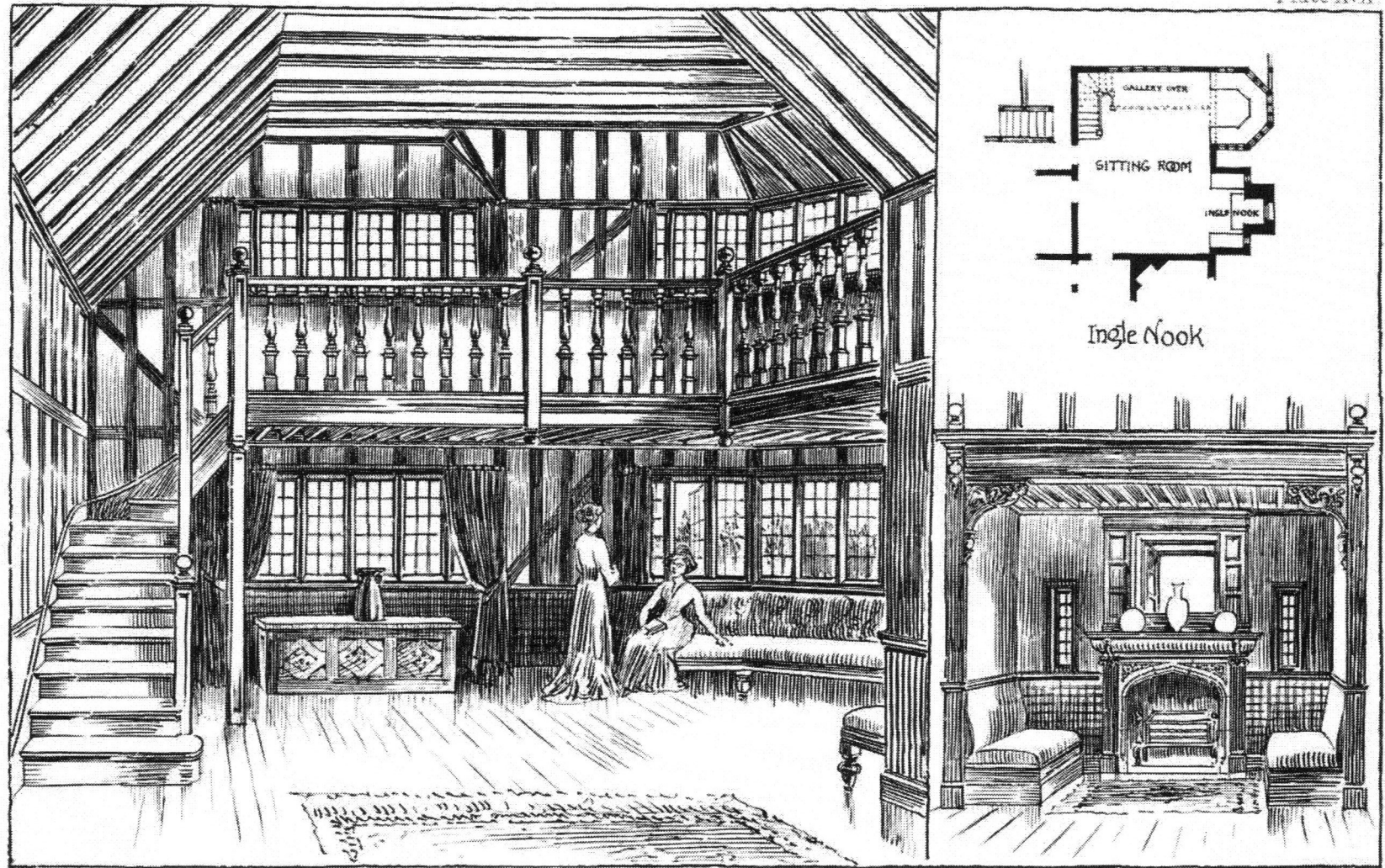

Plate XVII

GALLERY OVER

SITTING ROOM

INGLE NOOK

Ingle Nook

Plate XVIII.

Ground Floor Plan

Drawing Room

Conservatory

Dining Room

Hall

Library

Porch

Kitchen

Plate XIX.

Plate XX

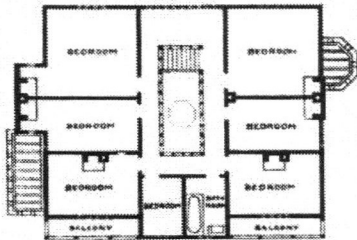

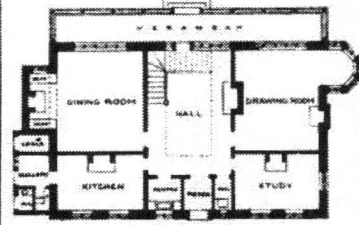

Plate XXI.

J. Akerman, Photo lith. London

Plate XXII

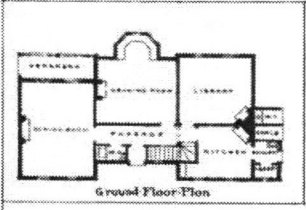

Ground Floor Plan

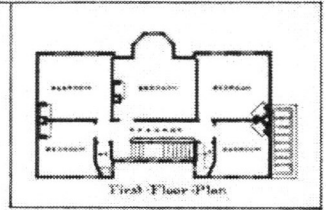

First Floor Plan

Plate XXIII.

"Photo-Tint", by J. Akerman, 8, Queen Square, W.C.

Plate XXIV

GROUND FLOOR
PLAN

KITCHEN

DINING ROOM

HALL · SITTING ROOM

VERANDAH

FIRST FLOOR
PLAN

BEDROOM

PASSAGE

BEDROOM

BEDROOM

BEDROOM

J. Akerman Photo-lith London

Plate XXX

Plate XXVI

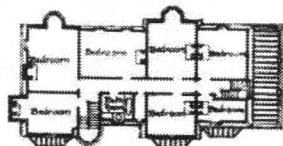

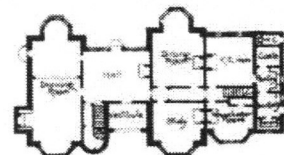

Plate XXVII

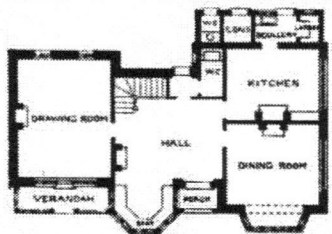

GROUND FLOOR PLAN.

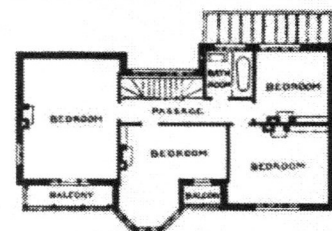

FIRST FLOOR PLAN.

Plate XXVIII

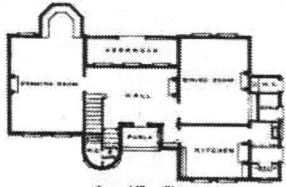

Ground Floor Plan.

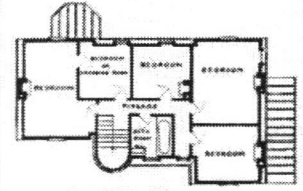

First Floor Plan

Plate XXIV

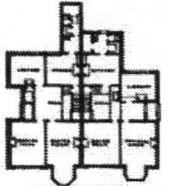

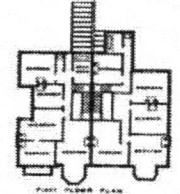

Plate XXX

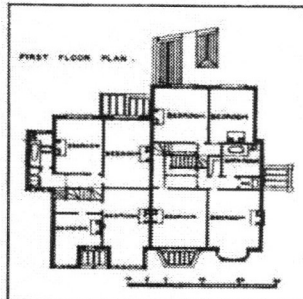

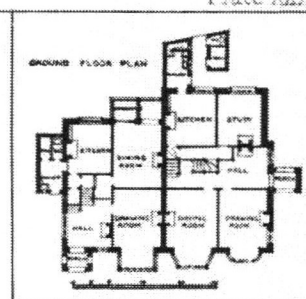

Plate XXXI

FIRST FLOOR PLAN

GROUND FLOOR PLAN

Plate XXXII

J. Akerman, Photo lith London

Plate XXIII

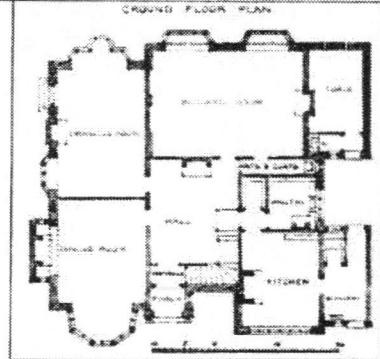

Plate XXXIV

Plate XXXV

FIRST FLOOR PLAN

GROUND FLOOR PLAN

Plate XXXVI.

Scale of feet

Library

Pantry

W.C.

Kitchen

Drawing Room

Hall

Dining Room

Porch

Ground Floor Plan

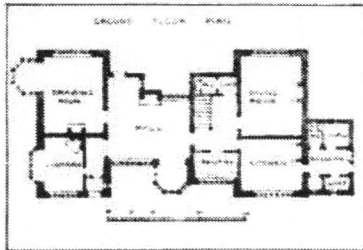

Plate XXXVII

Plate XXXVIII

Plate XXXIX

Plate XI.

Plate XLI

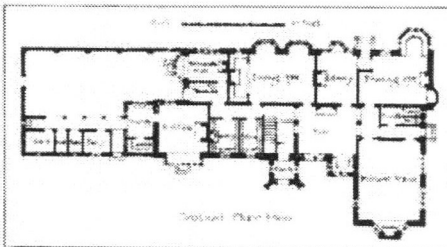

Plate XLII.

Plate XLII

Plate XLIV

Plate XLV.

J. Akerman Photo lith London

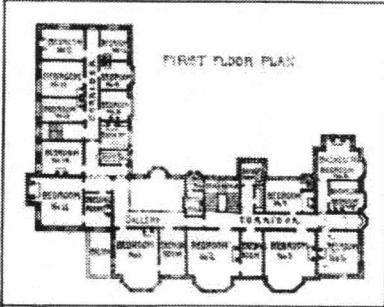

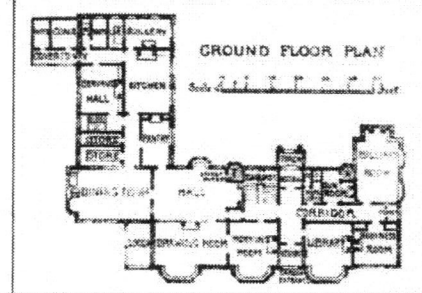

Plate XLVI.

Plate XLVII

www.ingramcontent.com/pod-product-compliance
Lightning Source LLC
Chambersburg PA
CBHW062049090426
42740CB00016B/3077